BIRBAL THE WISE

THE WICKED BARBER

BIRBAL WAS A MINISTER AT THE COURT OF EMPEROR AKBAR. BOTH, HINDUS AND MUSLIMS AT THE COURT, LIKED HIM FOR HIS READY WIT AND KEEN SENSE OF HUMOUR. HOWEVER, THERE WERE A FEW WHO ENVIED HIM.

THEY HATCHED A PLOT TO KILL HIM. WITH THIS IN VIEW, THEY MET THE EMPEROR'S BARBER TO ASK FOR HIS HELP.

HAJAM✳ SAHAB, IF YOU WILL DO US A SMALL FAVOUR, WE WILL GIVE YOU A BAG FULL OF GOLD.

WHAT DO YOU WANT ME TO DO?

BUZZ... BUZZ

REST ASSURED, I'LL TELL THE EMPEROR TOMORROW.

THE NEXT MORNING—

JAHANPANAH⊕, I HAVE OFTEN WONDERED...

WHY DO YOU HESITATE? BE FRANK, MY MAN. SPEAK UP!

JAHANPANAH, HAS IT EVER OCCURRED TO YOU THAT YOU ARE DOING NOTHING FOR THE WELFARE OF YOUR ANCESTORS?

✳ BARBER   ⊕ REFUGE OF THE WORLD.

BUT THEY ARE DEAD AND IN HEAVEN. HOW AM I TO KNOW WHAT THEY NEED?

YOU CAN SEND SOMEONE THERE TO FIND OUT.

INDEED! IT'S A GOOD IDEA! CAN YOU SUGGEST HOW IT'S TO BE DONE?

A THOUSAND BUNDLES OF HAY SHOULD BE PILED IN THE OPEN GROUND OUTSIDE THE CITY. AFTER A CHOSEN MAN ASCENDS THE PILE, IT MUST BE SET ALIGHT.

AND THE MAN WILL RISE STRAIGHT UP TO HEAVEN ALONG WITH THE SMOKE.

BUT WHO...?

WHO ELSE BUT THE WISE BIRBAL?

SO THAT'S IT! ONE MORE TRAP SET FOR MY TRUSTED FRIEND. BUT I CAN TRUST HIM TO GET OUT OF IT.

ALL RIGHT. THEN BIRBAL SHALL GO.

THAT EVENING, THE EMPEROR ANNOUNCED HIS PLAN AT COURT.

...AND BIRBAL, I HAVE CHOSEN YOU FOR THE TASK. PLEASE GO TO HEAVEN AND SEE IF MY ANCESTORS NEED ANYTHING.

?

BIRBAL IMMEDIATELY GOT A FEW TRUSTED WORKMEN TO DIG A TUNNEL FROM HIS HOUSE TO THE OPEN GROUND WHERE THE BUNDLES OF HAY WERE BEING PILED UP.

ON THE APPOINTED DAY, EVERYONE GATHERED TO SEE BIRBAL ASCEND TO HEAVEN.

I WOULD LIKE TO LIE DOWN HERE. PLEASE START PILING THE HAY AROUND ME.

BIRBAL HAD CHOSEN A SPOT NEAR THE ENTRANCE TO HIS TUNNEL WHICH HAD BEEN CLEVERLY CONCEALED BY A FEW BUNDLES OF HAY.

WHEN THE BUNDLES OF HAY BEGAN TO BURN, BIRBAL'S FRIENDS SHED TEARS...

POOR MAN! HOW CAN HE COME BACK ALIVE? HE WAS A GOOD AND NOBLE SOUL — A REAL FRIEND INDEED!

...BUT HIS ENEMIES REJOICED.

WE HAVE AT LAST GOT RID OF HIM. WE MUST CELEBRATE THE OCCASION.

MEANWHILE —

ONCE I REACH HOME, I WILL REMAIN THERE FOR A FEW MONTHS TILL I THINK OF A PLAN TO PUNISH THE BARBER.

SIX MONTHS LATER, WHEN BIRBAL ENTERED THE COURT, NO ONE RECOGNISED HIM.

WHO COULD THAT MAN BE? WHAT DOES HE WANT HERE?

AKBAR, HOWEVER, RE-COGNISED HIM IMMEDIATELY.

JUST AS I HAD ANTICIPATED... BIRBAL HAS ESCAPED, UNHURT.

JAHANPANAH, I COME STRAIGHT FROM HEAVEN.

IT IS GOOD TO SEE YOU AGAIN, BIRBAL.

HOW IS EVERY-BODY UP THERE? HOW IS MY FATHER?

THEY ARE ALL FINE AND HAVE ALL THE COMFORTS UP THERE. BUT THERE IS ONE THING THEY LACK— A GOOD BARBER...

...WHICH EXPLAINS MY UNCUT HAIR AND BEARD. YOUR FORE-FATHERS ARE UNHAPPY ABOUT THIS, AND WANT YOU TO SEND THEM A GOOD BARBER.

THAT SHOULD NOT BE DIFFICULT NOW THAT WE KNOW HOW THE JOURNEY CAN BE MADE. BUT WHO...

WHO ELSE BUT THE ROYAL BARBER! YOUR FATHER WAS PARTICULARLY FOND OF HIM.

GOOD. I WILL DO AS YOU SAY.

WHEN THE BARBER RECEIVED THE ORDERS, HE RAN TO THE COURTIERS WHO HAD PLOTTED AGAINST BIRBAL.

PLEASE DO SOMETHING TO SAVE ME, I BEG OF YOU.

WHAT CAN WE DO?

REALISING THAT HE WAS TRAPPED, THE FRIGHTENED BARBER TOOK TO HIS HEELS AND WAS NEVER HEARD OF AGAIN.

BEGUM RECONCILED

HUSSAIN KHAN, AS THE EMPEROR'S BROTHER-IN-LAW, YOU OUGHT TO BE THE MINISTER INSTEAD OF BIRBAL.

BUT THE EMPEROR DOES NOT THINK SO.

THIS TIME, THE PLOTTERS HAD DECIDED TO MAKE USE OF HUSSAIN KHAN, THE EMPEROR'S BROTHER-IN-LAW, TO ACHIEVE THEIR GOAL.

WHY DON'T YOU ASK YOUR SISTER TO PLEAD YOUR CASE WITH THE EMPEROR?

A GOOD IDEA. HOW STRANGE THAT I DIDN'T THINK OF IT EARLIER!

A FEW DAYS LATER —

BEGUM, YOU SEEM TO BE UPSET ABOUT SOMETHING. WON'T YOU CONFIDE IN ME?

THE NEXT DAY—

JAHANPANAH, YOU SEEM TROUBLED. WHAT IS THE MATTER?

IT'S MY BEGUM. SHE IS ANNOYED WITH ME AND REFUSES TO SEE ME.

GO BRING HER TO ME THIS MINUTE. ONLY YOU CAN DO IT.

IF YOU FAIL, YOU WILL LOSE YOUR POST. I WILL APPOINT HUSSAIN KHAN AS MY MINISTER. THAT WOULD PLEASE MY BEGUM.

SO THAT'S THEIR GAME THIS TIME!

BIRBAL WORE AN ABJECT LOOK, AS HE STOOD BEFORE THE BEGUM.

BEGUM SAHIBA, I COME WITH A MESSAGE FROM THE EMPEROR.

HE IS IN THE PALACE GARDEN. HE WANTS YOU TO • • •

JUST THEN A MESSENGER WALKED UP TO HIM.

WHAT IS IT?

THIS MESSAGE IS ONLY FOR YOUR EARS, HUZUR *

AS THE MESSENGER WHISPERED INTO BIRBAL'S EAR, THREE OF HIS WORDS WERE LOUD AND CLEAR.

BUZZ • • • BUZZ • • • SHE IS BEAUTIFUL • • •

BIRBAL TURNED TO THE BEGUM.

NOW THE WHOLE SITUATION HAS CHANGED. YOU NEED NOT COME, BEGUM SAHIBA.

SOON AFTER, BIRBAL LEFT—

WHAT! DID I NOT OVERHEAR SOMETHING ABOUT A BEAUTIFUL MAIDEN? PERHAPS THE EMPEROR DOES NOT WANT ME TO SEE HIM WITH HER.

BURNING WITH JEALOUS CURIOSITY, THE BEGUM HURRIED TOWARDS THE PALACE GARDEN.

SHE WAS SURPRISED TO SEE THE EMPEROR ALONE.

BEGUM! BUT YOU HAD PROMISED THAT YOU WOULD NOT COME!

THE DEAREST OBJECT

ONE DAY, FOR SOME REASON, AKBAR BECAME DISPLEASED WITH HIS BEGUM.

I ORDER YOU TO LEAVE THE PALACE WITHIN A DAY.

JAHANPANAH, HOW CAN I LIVE WITH-OUT YOU? PLEASE DON'T SEND ME AWAY.

I HAVE MADE UP MY MIND. YOU WILL HAVE TO GO. HOWEVER, YOU MAY TAKE WITH YOU THE OB-JECTS THAT ARE DEAR TO YOU.

AS THE DEJECTED BEGUM WONDERED WHAT TO DO, A THOUGHT SUDDENLY OCCURRED TO HER.

PERHAPS, BIRBAL CAN HELP ME.

SHE SENT FOR BIRBAL AND EXPLAINED THE SITUATION TO HIM.

HE SAID YOU COULD TAKE WHATEVER WAS DEAR TO YOU, DIDN'T HE?

WHEN BIRBAL LEFT AFTER TELLING THE BEGUM WHAT SHE SHOULD DO —

PACK MY BELONGINGS. I AM GOING HOME FOR A FEW DAYS.

WHEN ALL HER BELONG-INGS WERE PACKED —

NOW, TELL YOUR MASTER THAT I WOULD LIKE TO SEE HIM BEFORE I LEAVE.

WHEN AKBAR ARRIVED —

MAY I OFFER YOU A GLASS OF SHERBET, PLEASE?

I HAVE NO OBJECTION.

AFTER AKBAR DRANK THE SHERBET —

I FEEL SLEEPY.

LATER —

ARE THE PALANQUINS READY?

THEY ARE, BEGUM SAHIBA.

WITH THE SLEEPING EMPEROR IN ONE PALANQUIN AND THE BEGUM SAHIBA IN THE OTHER, THE PARTY LEFT AGRA...

...AND IN A FEW HOURS REACHED THE BEGUM'S FATHER'S HOUSE.

I AM PLEASED TO SEE YOU, DEAR. BUT WHY HAVE YOU COME AT SUCH AN ODD TIME?

FATHER, I WILL EXPLAIN EVERYTHING LATER. LET US FIRST MAKE AR- RANGEMENTS FOR THE EMPEROR'S STAY.

HE IS STILL ASLEEP.

HE WILL WAKE UP IN ANOTHER HOUR OR SO.

AN HOUR LATER —

WHERE AM I?

ISN'T THIS YOUR FATHER'S HOUSE? HOW DID I COME HERE?

JAHANPANAH, YOU HAD ORDERED ME TO LEAVE THE PALACE...

...BUT YOU HAD GIVEN ME PERMISSION TO CARRY AWAY ANYTHING THAT WAS DEAR TO ME. NOTHING IS MORE DEAR TO ME THAN YOU. SO, I BROUGHT YOU AWAY WITH ME.

WHAT?

AFTER THIS INCIDENT, THE BEGUM FELT EVER OBLIGED TO BIRBAL FOR RESTORING HER TO HER HUSBAND'S FAVOUR.

BIRBAL'S VISIT TO BURMA

HUSSAIN KHAN COULD NOT GIVE UP THE IDEA THAT HE OUGHT TO BE THE MINISTER AND NOT BIRBAL. SINCE HE COULD NOT INDUCE HIS SISTER TO SPEAK FOR HIM, HE ASKED THE COURTIERS TO SPEAK TO THE EMPEROR.

THEY WERE ONLY TOO GLAD TO DO SO.

JAHANPANAH! WE HAVE HAD A HINDU MINISTER FOR A LONG TIME. IS IT NOT FAIR TO GIVE HUSSAIN KHAN A CHANCE, NOW?

AKBAR THOUGHT FOR A WHILE.

IT SEEMS THESE PEOPLE ARE BENT ON MAKING HUSSAIN KHAN MY MINISTER. I MUST SETTLE THIS MATTER ONCE AND FOR ALL.

A FEW DAYS LATER —

THIS IS A SEALED LETTER, TO THE KING OF BURMA.

SINCE IT IS EXTREMELY IMPORTANT, I WANT BIRBAL AND HUSSAIN KHAN TO GO TO BURMA AND DELIVER IT PERSONALLY.

BIRBAL AND HUSSAIN KHAN SET OUT ON THE JOURNEY.

AT BURMA —

WE SEEK AN AUDIENCE WITH THE KING. WE HAVE AN URGENT MESSAGE FOR HIM FROM THE EMPEROR OF HINDUSTAN.*

* INDIA

THE KING WAS SURPRISED WHEN THE GUARD ANNOUNCED THE MESSAGE.

DOES THE EMPEROR HAVE EVIL DESIGNS ON BURMA?

SEND THEM IN.

BUT WHEN HE READ THE LETTER —

HOW CAN THIS BE? WHAT DOES IT MEAN?

HE TURNED TO HIS MINISTER —

MAKE ARRANGE- MENTS FOR THEIR STAY. KEEP A CLOSE WATCH ON THEM. SEE TO IT THAT THEY DON'T ESCAPE.

LATER, WHEN THEY WERE ALONE, THE KING CONFIDED IN HIS MINISTER.

THE EMPEROR OF HINDUSTAN WANTS ME TO HANG THESE TWO MEN ON THE NIGHT OF THE FULL MOON. WHAT DOES THAT MEAN?

THERE IS SOMETHING SUSPICIOUS IN IT. WHY COULDN'T HE HANG THEM IN AGRA?

PERHAPS THEY ARE POWERFUL MEN AT HIS COURT. AND HE DID NOT WANT ANYONE TO KNOW THAT THE EMPEROR HAD CAUSED THEM HARM.

IF THESE MEN DO HAVE BACKING AT THE COURT, THEN THOSE WHO WILL COME TO POWER AFTER AKBAR WILL BE ANGRY WITH US FOR KILLING THEIR LEADERS. WE MUST FIND OUT MORE ABOUT THEM.

BIRBAL AND HUSSAIN KHAN TOO HAD A SECRET DISCUSSION.

HUSSAIN KHAN, I DON'T KNOW THE CONTENTS OF THE LETTER. BUT FROM THE EXPRESSION ON THE KING'S FACE AND FROM HIS ORDER, I FEEL THAT WE ARE IN TROUBLE.

ABOUT THAT THERE'S NO DOUBT. OTHERWISE, WHY WOULD HE WANT TO POST SO MANY GUARDS TO KEEP WATCH ON US?

BIRBAL, YOU ARE A WISE MAN. PLEASE SAVE ME. I SHALL BE ETERNALLY OBLIGED TO YOU!

I WILL DO MY BEST. BUT REMEMBER TO TAKE A CUE FROM MY WORDS AND TO REPEAT THEM IF NECESSARY.

JUST THEN, THE DOOR OF THEIR ROOM OPENED AND IN CAME THE MINISTER.

HE CAME TO BIRBAL.

I UNDERSTAND, ONE OF YOU IS BIRBAL AND THE OTHER HUSSAIN KHAN. EMPEROR AKBAR HAS REQUESTED THAT BOTH OF YOU BE HANGED ON THE NIGHT OF THE FULL MOON. WHY?

OUR EMPEROR IS KIND AND JUST. PLEASE CARRY OUT HIS ORDERS.

HUSSAIN KHAN TURNED PALE WITH FEAR, BUT HE DID NOT FORGET TO TAKE THE CUE FROM BIRBAL.

YES, YOU MUST HANG US ON THE NIGHT OF THE FULL MOON.

THE BAFFLED MINISTER REPORTED THE MATTER TO HIS KING.

YOUR MAJESTY, I THINK THERE MUST BE SOME REASON WHY THESE MEN WANT TO BE HANGED ON THE NIGHT OF THE FULL MOON.

IF WE DON'T CARRY OUT THE ORDER, THE EMPEROR OF HINDUSTAN WILL BE ANGRY.

MEANWHILE, BIRBAL DISCUSSED HIS PLANS WITH HUSSAIN KHAN.

...WHEN THEY TAKE US TO THE GALLOWS, I WILL INSIST THAT I BE HANGED FIRST. YOU MUST DO THE SAME.

ON *THE NIGHT OF THE FULL MOON*—

YOUR MAJESTY! IT WAS I WHO HAD HANDED OVER THE EMPEROR'S LETTER TO YOU. KINDLY HANG ME FIRST.

I AM THE EMPEROR'S BROTHER-IN-LAW. I BEG OF YOU TO HANG ME FIRST.

THE MINISTER TURNED TO BIRBAL.

IF YOU TELL US WHY YOU ARE SO ANXIOUS TO BE HANGED, WE WILL HANG YOU FIRST.

IS THAT A PROMISE?

YES.

IT IS DESTINED THAT THE ONE WHO IS KILLED HERE TODAY WILL BECOME THE KING OF THIS COUNTRY, IN HIS NEXT BIRTH.

THE KING HAD HURRIED CONSULTATIONS WITH HIS MINISTERS.

I CERTAINLY DO NOT WANT ANYONE EXCEPT MY SON TO BE THE KING OF THIS COUNTRY.

I SUGGEST WE WRITE TO THE EMPEROR THAT SINCE HE HAS NOT GIVEN ANY INDICATION OF THE NATURE OF THE CRIME COMMITTED BY THESE MEN, WE CANNOT HANG THEM.

WHEN THE DECISION WAS ANNOUNCED—

YOUR MAJESTY! IT IS VERY UNFAIR ON THE PART OF THE MINISTER TO GO BACK ON HIS PROMISE.

LET A CLOSE WATCH BE KEPT ON THESE MEN TO ENSURE THAT THEY DO NOT GET KILLED OR THAT THEY DO NOT COMMIT SUICIDE.

JUST AS BIRBAL HAD EXPECTED, THEY WERE ESCORTED TO THE BORDER OF AKBAR'S EMPIRE.

WHEN THE TWO REACHED EMPEROR AKBAR'S COURT—

DID YOU ENJOY THE TRIP TO BURMA?

YES, JAHANPANAH! WE WERE TREATED WITH GREAT HONOUR AND ESCORTED BACK.

LATER, WHEN HUSSAIN KHAN TOLD AKBAR ALL THAT HAD HAPPENED IN BURMA—

WOULD YOU LIKE TO BE MY MINISTER, HUSSAIN KHAN?

NO, JAHANPANAH. THAT POST CAN ONLY BELONG TO BIRBAL. HIS WISDOM IS UNMATCHED.

SUBSCRIBE NOW!

TINKLE COMBO MAGAZINE + DIGEST
1 year subscription

Pay only ₹~~1200~~ ₹880!

FREE
2 Time Compass DVDs worth ₹598

TINKLE MAGAZINE
1 year subscription

Pay only ₹~~480~~ ₹380!

I would like a one year subscription for

TINKLE COMBO ☐   **TINKLE MAGAZINE** ☐

(Please tick the appropriate box)

YOUR DETAILS*

Name: .... Date of Birth: |_|_| / |_|_| / |_|_|_|_|

Address: ....

.... City: .... Pin: |_|_|_|_|_|_| State: ....

School: .... Class: ....

Tel: .... Mobile: + 91 - |_|_|_|_|_|_|_|_|_|_|_|

Email: .... Signature: ....

PAYMENT OPTIONS

☐ Cheque /DD:

Please find enclosed Cheque /DD no. |_|_|_|_|_|_|_| drawn in favour of 'ACK Media Direct Pvt. Ltd.'

at .... (bank) for the amount .... ,

dated |_|_| / |_|_| / |_|_|_|_| and send it to: IBH Books & Magazines Distributers Pvt. Ltd., Arch No. 30, West Approach, Below Mahalaxmi Bridge, Mahalaxmi (W), Mumbai - 400034.

☐ Pay Cash on Delivery: Pay cash on delivery of the first issue to the postman. (Additional charge of ₹50 applicable)

☐ Pay by money order: Pay by money order in favour of "ACK Media Direct Pvt. Ltd."

☐ Online subscription: Please visit: www.amarchitrakatha.com

For any queries or further information: Email: customerservice@ack-media.com or Call: 022-40497435 / 36

BIRBAL THE CLEVER

TALES OF BIRBAL

The route to your roots

BIRBAL THE CLEVER

Birbal had proved himself to be the most reliable minister at court, time and again. He dispensed justice, dealt diplomatically with other rulers, led military expeditions and composed poetry. In addition, he also rescued Akbar from the dangers of arrogance and unfettered power. Most importantly, he made the Great Mughal laugh.

Script
Meera Ugra

Illustrations
Ram Waeerkar

Editor
Anant Pai

THE PUNISHMENT

AFTER THE DAY'S WORK WAS DONE, AKBAR, THE MUGHAL EMPEROR, LIKED TO PASS A FEW LIGHT-HEARTED MOMENTS WITH HIS COURTIERS. HE OFTEN POSED STRANGE QUESTIONS TO PROVOKE AMUSING REPLIES.

ONE MORNING, AS AKBAR WAS GETTING DRESSED, HIS GRANDSON CAME RUNNING TO HIM.

BABA, BABA, THERE IS SOMETHING BLACK IN YOUR MOUSTACHE! BEND DOWN, AND I WILL TAKE IT OUT!

O...OU...OUCH!

THAT WAS NAUGHTY OF YOU! WHY DID YOU DO IT?

HA! HA! BABA! I FOOLED YOU!

NOW, GO AND PLAY. I'VE GOT WORK TO DO.

AKBAR LEFT FOR HIS DARBAR.

AHA, TODAY I HAVE A PROBLEM WHICH WILL BAFFLE EVERYONE — EVEN BIRBAL, MY WITTY MINISTER! HE THINKS HE HAS ALL THE ANSWERS, BUT HE'LL BE FOXED THIS TIME!

SOMEONE PULLED A HAIR FROM MY MOUSTACHE THIS MORNING. I WANT HIM PUNISHED!

CAN ANYONE HERE THINK OF SUITABLE PUNISHMENT FOR THIS DEED?

AFTER A MOMENT'S SHOCKED SILENCE, THERE WAS A CHORUS OF SUGGESTIONS.

THE MAN SHOULD BE FLOGGED A THOUSAND TIMES!

THAT'S TOO MILD! THE SCOUN-DREL SHOULD BE IMPRISONED FOR LIFE!

HANG HIM, JAHANPANAH!

THE EMPEROR TURNED TO BIRBAL.

WHY ARE YOU SO QUIET, BIRBAL? ARE YOU STUCK FOR IDEAS?

NO, JAHAN-PANAH. BUT IT'S A BIT AWKWARD. PERHAPS I SHOULD SPEAK TO YOU IN PRIVATE....

NO, BIRBAL! LET EVERYONE HEAR WHAT YOU HAVE TO SAY.

THE GUILTY PERSON DESERVES ONE LOUD, RESOUNDING KISS!

BIRBAL HAS GONE OUT OF HIS MIND!

WHAT!

AS USUAL, MY CLEVER MINISTER HAS GOT THE BETTER OF ME!

BIRBAL, EXPLAIN YOURSELF. WHY THIS STRANGE PUNISHMENT?

ONLY A CHILD WOULD DARE TO INDULGE IN SUCH A PRANK. AND THAT CHILD COULD ONLY BE YOUR GRAND-SON!

HA! HA! CLEVER BIRBAL!

THE MOST BEAUTIFUL CHILD IN AGRA

AKBAR WAS VERY FOND OF HIS GRANDCHILDREN.

ONCE —

ISN'T PRINCE KHURRAM MORE HANDSOME THAN ANY OTHER CHILD AROUND?

YES, JAHANPANAH!

WITHOUT A DOUBT, JAHANPANAH!

YOU ARE SILENT, BIRBAL? DON'T YOU AGREE WITH ME?

IT IS A DIFFICULT QUESTION, JAHANPANAH. FOR THERE IS NO REAL TEST FOR BEAUTY.

WHY NOT? WHO WOULD CALL A ROSE UGLY OR A CROW BEAUTIFUL?

HMM... YOU HAVE A POINT THERE, JAHANPANAH.

YOU DON'T SEEM CONVINCED. ALL RIGHT, WE'LL HAVE A CONTEST TOMORROW.

EACH OF YOU SHALL BRING ALONG A CHILD. I AM SURE WE WILL THEN BE ABLE TO DECIDE WHICH AMONG THEM IS THE MOST BEAUTIFUL.

THE NEXT DAY, AKBAR FOUND THAT THE NOBLES HAD FOLLOWED HIS INSTRUCTIONS —

HMM. THAT CHILD'S EYES ARE A BIT SMALL FOR HIS FACE. AND THAT ONE THERE LOOKS A BIT TOO FAT.

I STILL THINK MY KHURRAM LOOKS BETTER THAN ALL OF THEM. BUT, BIRBAL, WHY HAVEN'T YOU BROUGHT A CHILD?

JAHANPANAH, I COULD NOT FIND A CHILD WHO IS PERFECT IN EVERY FEATURE. GIVE ME A FEW MORE DAYS.

SOMETIME LATER —

BIRBAL, I AM STILL WAITING. HOW MUCH LONGER WILL YOU TAKE?

MY SEARCH IS STILL ON, JAHANPANAH.

THEN, ONE DAY —

JAHANPANAH, AT LAST I HAVE FOUND THE MOST BEAUTIFUL CHILD IN AGRA.

HAVE YOU BROUGHT IT HERE?

NO, I'M AFRAID THE MOTHER WILL NOT PART WITH HER SON, FOR FEAR AN EVIL EYE MAY BE CAST ON HIM. WE'LL HAVE TO GO TO HIS HOUSE.

ALL RIGHT, I AM VERY CURIOUS TO SEE THIS CHILD. WE WILL DRESS LIKE ORDINARY CITIZENS AND GO.

TAKING ONLY A FEW COMPANIONS WITH THEM, AKBAR AND BIRBAL WENT OUT IN DISGUISE. THEY WALKED FOR A LONG TIME.

HOW MUCH FURTHER IS IT?

WE HAVE COME A LONG WAY. WHERE IS BIRBAL TAKING US TO?

THE HOUSES ARE BEGINNING TO LOOK MORE AND MORE SHABBY AND DIRTY. I HOPE BIRBAL KNOWS WHAT HE IS DOING!

FINALLY, BIRBAL STOPPED.

THAT'S WHERE THE CHILD LIVES, MY LORD. WE'LL WATCH HIM FROM A DISTANCE.

BUT WHERE IS HE, BIRBAL?

WHY, THERE HE IS!

ALL EYES TURNED TOWARDS THE "MOST BEAUTIFUL CHILD IN AGRA".

THAT CHILD! IS THIS ANOTHER OF YOUR PRANKS, BIRBAL? THIS IS THE UGLIEST CHILD I HAVE EVER COME ACROSS!

I BEG OF YOU TO BE A LITTLE MORE PATIENT, JAHANPANAH.

JUST THEN THE CHILD STUMBLED AND FELL.

O....O....A....

HIS MOTHER RUSHED OUT OF THE HUT.

OH—MY CHILD!

SHE PICKED HIM UP AND CARESSED HIM.

MY SWEETHEART, MY ANGEL! MY LOVELY ONE FELL DOWN! I'LL BEAT THE GROUND! HURTING MY MOON SO!

HOW CAN SHE LOVE THIS UGLY CHILD? HE IS UTTERLY REPULSIVE. DON'T YOU THINK SO, FRIEND?

YES, IMAGINE CALLING THE CHILD A MOON! UGH!

THE WOMAN JUMPED UP TO FACE THEM.

WHAT? WHAT DID YOU SAY? JUST SAY IT AGAIN.

WE SPOKE THE TRUTH. THIS CHILD IS...!

BE QUIET! THERE'S NO NEED TO REPEAT SUCH LIES! YOU MUST BE BLIND OR STUPID — GO AND SEARCH ALL OF AGRA AND SEE IF YOU CAN FIND A LOVELIER CHILD. GO AWAY NOW, OR I'LL GIVE YOU A PROPER THRASHING!

THEY BEAT A HASTY RETREAT.

I UNDERSTAND, BIRBAL. EVERY CHILD IS SURPASSINGLY BEAUTIFUL IN THE EYES OF ITS PARENTS...

...OR ITS GRANDPARENTS!

THE WHIM OF A CHILD

EMPEROR AKBAR AND HIS COURTIERS WERE ASSEMBLED IN COURT.

I DON'T SEE BIRBAL HERE TODAY. WHAT COULD HAVE HAPPENED TO HIM?

JUST THEN, BIRBAL CAME IN —

A THOUSAND APOLOGIES, JAHAN-PANAH. I AM INDEED ASHAMED TO HAVE ARRIVED LATE BEFORE YOUR AUGUST PRESENCE.

IT IS ALL RIGHT, BIRBAL. SOMETHING EXTRAORDINARY MUST HAVE DELAYED YOU.

WHEN BIRBAL DIDN'T REPLY, AKBAR PRESSED FURTHER.

WHAT WAS IT, BIRBAL? WHAT MADE YOU SO LATE?

I WAS DETAINED BY... ER...

9

DETAINED BY WHAT?

IT WAS LIKE THIS, JAHANPANAH — MY SON ... WELL ... YOU SEE ... HE IS ONLY FOUR YEARS OLD. HIS TOY BROKE AND HE WOULDN'T LET ME GO TILL I HAD REPAIRED IT.

SO BIRBAL CAME LATE BECAUSE HE COULDN'T COPE WITH HIS SON! HA! HA!

HA! HA!

BIRBAL MET HIS MATCH TODAY IN A CHILD! HA! HA!

BIRBAL BEATEN BY A MERE CHILD! HA! HA!

EXCUSE ME, JAHANPANAH, BUT SOMETIMES EVEN THE GODS ARE HELPLESS IN THE FACE OF A CHILD'S OBSTINACY.

BUT THAT'S ABSURD! BRING YOUR SON HERE, AND I'LL TACKLE HIM IN NO TIME.

SO BIRBAL'S SON WAS BROUGHT BEFORE THE EMPEROR.

WELL, CHILD, WOULD YOU LIKE TO EAT SOMETHING?

HUZOOR, I WOULD....

THE MAN WHO BROUGHT ILL LUCK

THE DAY'S WORK IN AKBAR'S PALACE BEGAN VERY EARLY IN THE MORNING.

THERE GOES GULSHAN, THE INAUSPICIOUS ONE. WE HAVE SEEN HIS FACE THE FIRST THING THIS MORNING. WE WILL NOT GET ANY FOOD TODAY.

OR, PERHAPS, A WORSE CALAMITY WILL BEFALL US!

THAT DAY, THE EMPEROR WOKE UP EARLIER THAN USUAL.

IS SOMEONE THERE?

THERE IS NO ONE ELSE AROUND. I DON'T WANT TO BE THE FIRST PERSON HE SEES THIS MORNING BUT....

GULSHAN WENT IN RELUCTANTLY.

JAHANPANAH....

MY SLIPPERS! GIVE ME MY SLIPPERS!

OH! IT'S THAT SERVANT WHOM EVERY-ONE AVOIDS!

13

SEND THE OTHER SERVANTS IN TO HELP ME GET DRESSED!

YES, HUZOOR.

A LITTLE LATER —

JAHANPANAH! PRINCE KHURRAM IS VERY ILL AND HAS BEEN CRYING FOR YOU.

I'LL COME AT ONCE!

THE EMPEROR SPENT A FEW ANXIOUS HOURS BY THE CHILD'S BED. THEN —

THANK GOD, THE FEVER HAS COME DOWN!

JAHANPANAH, THE CRISIS IS OVER; YOU SHOULD REST NOW.

AS AKBAR WAS GOING TO HIS CHAMBERS TO HAVE A LATE BREAKFAST —

JAHANPANAH, THE BURMESE AMBASSADOR HAS BEEN WAITING FOR AN AUDIENCE ALL MORNING.

YES, YES, I'LL COME AT ONCE.

LATER, JUST AS AKBAR WAS BIDDING THE AMBASSADOR FAREWELL, A MINISTER APPROACHED.

JAHANPANAH, MAY I HAVE A WORD WITH YOU IN PRIVATE? IT'S EXTREMELY URGENT.

I BRING BAD NEWS. THERE HAS BEEN A REBELLION.

A REBELLION! WE MUST ACT IMMEDIATELY. CALL THE COMMANDER IN CHARGE OF THE AREA!

THEY HELD CONSULTATIONS. IT WAS NEARLY EVENING WHEN THEY FINISHED.

I AM SO TIRED AND I HAVE HAD NOTHING TO EAT ALL DAY!

I'LL HAVE SOME REFRESHMENTS SENT IN IMMEDIATELY, JAHAN-PANAH.

BUT WHEN AKBAR SAT DOWN TO EAT—

A...AAH! I HAVE A PIERCING PAIN IN THE STOMACH...CALL MY PHYSICIAN!

WITHIN MINUTES, THE PHYSICIAN ARRIVED—

JAHANPANAH, PLEASE DO NOT EAT ANY-THING. YOU CAN DRINK SOME FRUIT JUICE, THOUGH.

A...AH... ALL RIGHT.

WHAT A DAY IT HAS BEEN! CAN GULSHAN HAVE BEEN THE CAUSE OF MY TROUBLES?

TORMENTED BY PAIN, FATIGUE AND HUNGER, AKBAR MADE A RASH DECISION.

SUCH A MAN IS A THREAT TO ALL THOSE AROUND HIM. HE SHOULD NOT LIVE!

THE NEXT DAY, THE WHOLE COURT WAS BUZZING WITH THE NEWS —

THE INAUSPICIOUS ONE IS TO BE EXECUTED!

THAT'S A GOOD THING! I GET VERY WORRIED WHENEVER I SEE GULSHAN.

BUT BIRBAL WAS DISTURBED.

I MUST MAKE THE EMPEROR SEE REASON. THE POOR MAN HAS COMMITTED NO CRIME!

JAHANPANAH, I WANT TO APPEAL TO YOU ON GULSHAN'S BEHALF. TO PROVE HIS INNOCENCE, CAN I ASK HIM A FEW QUESTIONS IN YOUR PRESENCE?

ALL RIGHT, BIRBAL. GO AHEAD.

GULSHAN WAS CALLED IN.

TELL ME, GULSHAN, WHOM DID YOU MEET YESTERDAY WHEN YOU STARTED YOUR DAILY DUTIES IN THE MORNING?

THERE WAS NO ONE AROUND, HUZOOR, I DID NOT MEET ANYONE.

THEN WHOM DID YOU SEE FIRST OF ALL, GULSHAN?

I SAW EMPEROR AKBAR.

16

JAHANPANAH, YOU CLAIM THE SIGHT OF THIS MAN'S FACE RESULTED IN YOUR TROUBLES YESTERDAY...

...BUT WHAT IF HE WERE TO CLAIM THAT THE SIGHT OF YOUR FACE WILL CAUSE THE LOSS OF HIS LIFE!

WHOSE FATE IS WORSE AND WHO IS RESPONSIBLE?

YOU ARE RIGHT. I WAS LOOKING AT IT ONLY FROM MY POINT OF VIEW.

YOU HAVE SAVED ME FROM PUNISHING AN INNOCENT PERSON, BIRBAL. RELEASE THE POOR MAN.

THE OBEDIENT HUSBAND

ONE DAY, AKBAR AND BIRBAL WERE GOING AROUND THE TOWN IN DISGUISE.

THEY HEARD A WOMAN LOUDLY SCOLDING HER HUSBAND.

YOU FOOL! YOU GOOD-FOR-NOTHING OAF! GO AWAY AND DON'T COME BACK, TILL YOU'VE DONE THE WORK.

WHY DO YOU THINK SUCH A STRONG, HEFTY MAN WOULD TAKE THOSE WORDS SO MEEKLY?

WIVES GENERALLY ORDER THEIR HUSBANDS AROUND, JAHANPANAH. THAT'S MARRIAGE FOR YOU.

AKBAR WAS NOT CONVINCED. HE DECIDED TO CONDUCT AN EXPERIMENT. SO THE NEXT DAY, HE SUMMONED ALL THE MARRIED MEN OF AGRA.

THE EMPEROR WANTS TO KNOW HOW MANY MEN IN THIS GATHER-ING OBEY THEIR WIVES' COMMANDS.

THOSE WHO DO WILL PLEASE GO TO THE RIGHT, AND THOSE WHO DO NOT, WILL GO TO THE LEFT.

THERE WAS A SCRAMBLE.

THEN A FEW MOMENTS LATER, EVERYONE HAD GONE TOWARDS THE RIGHT, EXCEPT FOR ONE SOLITARY PERSON.

AH! THERE IS AT LEAST ONE WISE MAN WHO DOES NOT FOLLOW HIS WIFE'S COMMANDS. I MUST REWARD HIM!

WAIT, JAHANPANAH! PLEASE LET ME ASK HIM ONE QUESTION FIRST.

THE EMPEROR IS PLEASED WITH YOU, YOUNG MAN. AND HE WANTS TO HONOUR YOU. BUT, FIRST, YOU MUST ANSWER ONE QUESTION...

...TELL ME, WHY DID YOU GO TO THE LEFT?

WELL... SIR... BECAUSE MY WIFE HAD TOLD ME TO KEEP AWAY FROM THE CROWDS. AND SO...

...WHEN EVERYONE MOVED TO THE RIGHT I REMEMBERED HER INSTRUCTIONS AND MOVED TO THE LEFT!

HA! HA!

HA! HA!

THE SEARCH FOR BIRBAL

THERE WERE OCCASIONS WHEN AKBAR GOT ANGRY WITH BIRBAL. ONE DAY, AKBAR BANISHED HIM FROM HIS COURT.

BIRBAL WENT HOME, AND WONDERED WHAT HE SHOULD DO NEXT.

IF I STAY HERE, THE EMPEROR MAY GIVE ME SOME HEAVIER PUNISHMENT. FOR THERE ARE MANY WHO ARE WAITING FOR AN OPPORTUNITY TO POISON HIS MIND AGAINST ME.

BUT IF I GO AWAY TO MY JAGIR, HE CAN EASILY RECALL ME. I MUST GO TO AN UNKNOWN PLACE, SO THAT HE WILL REALLY MISS ME.

AFTER A FEW WEEKS —

LIFE IS SO DULL WITHOUT BIRBAL'S QUICK WIT. HE WAS SO HONEST AND FEARLESS.

HE SENT HIS MESSENGERS TO LOOK FOR BIRBAL. BUT —

JAHANPANAH, WE HAVE LOOKED EVERY-WHERE. NO ONE KNOWS WHERE HE IS.

HMM. HE IS NEITHER IN AGRA NOR IN HIS JAGIR! HE MUST BE HIDING IN SOME OUT-OF-THE-WAY VILLAGE!

I MUST THINK OF A NOVEL WAY TO LOCATE HIM.

A FEW DAYS LATER, ALL THE VILLAGE CHIEFS RECEIVED A ROYAL COMMAND—

THE EMPEROR COM-MANDS OUR PRESENCE IN AGRA WITHIN FIFTEEN DAYS. AS WE GO THERE, WE MUST WALK PARTLY IN THE SHADE AND PARTLY IN THE SUN.

WHAT AN EXTRAORDINARY COMMAND! HOW CAN ONE DO THAT?

FIFTEEN DAYS LATER, AKBAR WATCHED THE CHIEFS ARRIVING.

ONE OF THEM WAS WALKING VERY CONFIDENTLY.

AHA! HE IS ACTUALLY WALKING PARTLY IN THE SHADE AND PARTLY IN THE SUN!

BRING THAT MAN HERE!

HOW DID YOU THINK OF THIS IDEA? SPEAK THE TRUTH.

JAHANPANAH, A FEW WEEKS AGO, A FRIEND OF A FRIEND OF MINE ARRIVED AT MY VILLAGE. HE IS MY GUEST. IT WAS HIS IDEA.

WHAT IS HIS NAME? SPEAK UP WITHOUT FEAR AND YOU WILL BE REWARDED.

WELL...MY LORD ...HIS NAME IS BIRBAL. BUT...HE SAID THAT SINCE HE WAS IN ROYAL DIS-FAVOUR....

DON'T WORRY ABOUT THAT. I PARDONED HIM LONG AGO. TELL HIM TO RETURN TO COURT.

AND BIRBAL REGAINED HIS PLACE IN AKBAR'S COURT.

THE LINGUIST

ONE DAY, A STRANGER ARRIVED AT AKBAR'S COURT.

JAHANPANAH, I CAN SPEAK PERSIAN, ARABIC, SANSKRIT, CHINESE AND LATIN.

WHERE HAVE YOU COME FROM, STRANGER?

THEY SAY A MAN'S LANGUAGE IS THE SUREST CLUE TO HIS ORIGIN. CAN THE WISE MEN OF YOUR COURT ANSWER YOUR QUESTION?

SEVERAL SCHOLARS QUESTIONED HIM IN VARIOUS LANGUAGES —

JAHANPANAH, HE SPEAKS MANY LANGUAGES FLUENTLY!

AND HIS DICTION AND COMMAND OVER EACH LANGUAGE IS PERFECT.

AKBAR TURNED TO BIRBAL —

WELL, BIRBAL, YOU'VE BEEN DEEP IN THOUGHT. SURELY YOU'VE DISCOVERED WHERE THIS MAN HAILS FROM?

I NEED A LITTLE MORE TIME, JAHANPANAH. PERHAPS BY TOMORROW I'LL BE ABLE TO TELL YOU.

LATER, BIRBAL CALLED A SERVANT AND GAVE HIM INSTRUCTIONS.

FOLLOW THAT STRANGER AND FIND OUT WHERE HE IS STAYING. THEN TONIGHT....

THAT NIGHT, A SHADOWY FIGURE QUIETLY SLIPPED INTO THE ROOM WHERE THE STRANGER WAS SLEEPING ...

... QUICKLY SPRINKLED A LITTLE WATER ON THE MAN...

...AND GLIDED OUT AS QUIETLY AS IT HAD COME. THE MAN WOKE UP WITH A START.

O!*!*!*!*!

THE NEXT DAY IN COURT —

THE STRANGER COMES FROM GUJARAT, JAHANPANAH.

OH! HOW DID HE GUESS?

WELL, IS IT TRUE, STRANGER?

Y... YES, JAHAN-PANAH. BUT HOW DID HE FIND OUT?

THE WHOLE COURT WAS EAGER TO HEAR THE ANSWER. BIRBAL EXPLAINED —

JAHANPANAH, I TOLD MY SERVANT TO SPRINKLE A LITTLE WATER ON OUR VISITOR AS HE SLEPT, AND I WAITED OUTSIDE, LISTENING CLOSELY.

IN MOMENTS OF PAIN, SURPRISE OR ANGER, A MAN USES HIS MOTHER-TONGUE. AND SO, WHEN I FOUND HIM MUMBLING IN GUJARATI, THE MYSTERY WAS SOLVED!

THE GREATER FOOL

ONCE AKBAR HAD ASKED BIRBAL TO MAKE A LIST OF FOOLS. SO BIRBAL WENT THROUGH THE STREETS OF AGRA LOOKING FOR FOOLS.

MEANWHILE, A MERCHANT ARRIVED AT THE COURT AND BOWED LOW BEFORE AKBAR.

YOUR MAJESTY, I SELL HORSES OF THE FINEST BREED. I HAVE BROUGHT ONE AS A SAMPLE. IT WOULD GIVE ME GOOD FORTUNE IF YOU JUST GAVE IT A GLANCE.

HORSES WERE AKBAR'S WEAKNESS. HE HAD THOUSANDS OF THEM IN HIS STABLE, BUT THE PROSPECT OF BUYING SOME MORE FINE STEEDS ALWAYS APPEALED TO HIM. HE INSPECTED THE HORSE PERSONALLY.

THAT IS A FINE SPECIMEN!

YOUR MAJESTY, I HAVE A HUNDRED SUCH HORSES. WOULD YOU LIKE TO BUY ALL OF THEM?

YES! WHEN CAN YOU BRING THEM?

JAHANPANAH, BUT FOR THE HEAVY EXPENSE I WOULD HAVE BROUGHT THEM WITH ME.

GIVE ME A LAKH OF GOLD COINS AND I WILL COME BACK WITH THEM IN A FORTNIGHT.

ONE LAKH OF GOLD COINS! OH, ALL RIGHT.

THE TREASURER WAS SUMMONED AND, RECEIVING THE MONEY, THE MERCHANT LEFT.

AH! THERE IS BIRBAL! I MUST SHOW HIM THIS FINE HORSE!

LOOK AT THIS FINE HORSE, BIRBAL! I HAVE JUST GIVEN THE MERCHANT A LAKH OF GOLD COINS FOR A HUNDRED SUCH HORSES.

YOU MEAN... YOU GAVE HIM THAT AMOUNT IN ADVANCE?

YES, OF COURSE! THE HORSES ARE CHEAP EVEN AT THAT PRICE. LET'S GO IN, NOW.

BUT, JAHANPANAH, DID THE MAN HAVE SUITABLE REFERENCES? OR DO YOU KNOW HIS ADDRESS? DID SOMEONE AT THE COURT STAND GUARANTEE FOR HIM?

NO...NO! BUT HE LOOKED HONEST ENOUGH. HE WILL COME BACK, BIRBAL. TELL ME NOW, HOW IS THE LIST OF FOOLS COMING ALONG?

IT IS ALMOST READY, JAHANPANAH. I HAVE JUST ONE MORE NAME TO ADD TO IT.

WELL, LET ME SEE IT THEN.

I'LL SHOW IT TO YOU IN A MOMENT.

BIRBAL STEPPED ASIDE TO WRITE ONE MORE NAME AND CAME BACK ALMOST IMMEDIATELY.

HERE IT IS, JAHANPANAH.

WHAT IS THIS? HOW DARE YOU, BIRBAL! WHY IS MY NAME ON THIS LIST?

I BEG YOUR PARDON, JAHANPANAH. BUT YOU HAVE JUST GIVEN AN UNKNOWN PERSON A LAKH OF GOLD COINS. WHAT ELSE CAN I CALL IT BUT AN ACT OF FOOLISHNESS?

BUT...HOW ARE YOU SO SURE? THE MATTER IS NOT CLOSED YET. WHAT IF HE COMES BACK WITHIN A FORTNIGHT WITH THE HORSES?

IN THAT CASE, I'LL TAKE OFF YOUR NAME FROM THE TOP OF THE LIST, JAHANPANAH...

... AND WRITE HIS NAME THERE!

AKBAR COULDN'T HELP LAUGHING. AND ONCE MORE BIRBAL HAD GOT AWAY WITH A CHEEKY ANSWER.

THOSE WHO CANNOT SEE

ONCE AKBAR HAD A CENSUS OF BLIND MEN TAKEN. BIRBAL WAS WITH HIM WHEN HE RECEIVED THE REPORT.

BIRBAL, THE BEGUM WANTS TO GIVE ALMS TO ALL THE BLIND PERSONS IN THE CITY. IT WAS EASY TO MAKE A LIST OF THEM BECAUSE THEY ARE SO FEW!

BUT, JAHANPANAH, THOSE WHO CANNOT SEE ARE MORE IN NUMBER THAN THOSE WHO CAN SEE!

DON'T BE SILLY, BIRBAL. MY MEN HAVE MADE A CAREFUL CHECK, AND YOU ARE WRONG.

THEY FORGOT TO INCLUDE THOSE WHO HAVE SIGHT AND YET CANNOT SEE, JAHAN-PANAH.

LOOK, BIRBAL, LET'S HAVE NO MORE OF YOUR JOKES.

YOU'LL SEE WHAT I MEAN, QUITE SOON, JAHANPANAH. JUST GIVE ME A FEW DAYS.

A FEW DAYS LATER, IN THE CITY'S MAIN STREET—

WHAT A CURIOUS SIGHT! WHAT IS HAPPENING HERE?

OH! IT'S BIRBAL!

HE'S UP TO SOME NEW GAME. LET'S GO NEARER AND SEE.

BIRBAL, WHAT ARE YOU DOING?

YES, WHAT IS THIS, BIRBAL?

TELL US!

START WRITING DOWN - NUMBER ONE, TWO, THREE ...

SOON, MORE AND MORE CURIOUS PEOPLE ARRIVED.

WHAT ARE YOU DOING BIRBAL?

WHAT ARE YOU UP TO?

BIRBAL PAID NO ATTENTION, BUT WENT ON DICTATING NUMBERS TO HIS CLERK.

SEVENTY-TWO, SEVENTY-THREE, SEVENTY-FOUR ....

HAS HE GONE CRAZY?

LOOKS LIKE IT! POOR MAN!

AFTER SOME TIME, EMPEROR AKBAR PASSED BY. HE, TOO, STOPPED.

BIRBAL, WHAT IS ALL THIS! WHAT ARE YOU DOING?

IGNORING THE EMPEROR, BIRBAL AGAIN INSTRUCTED HIS CLERK —

THAT WILL BE TWO HUNDRED AND FIFTY!

BIRBAL! WHAT SORT OF AN ANSWER IS THIS?

I AM STRINGING A CHARPOY, JAHANPANAH. AND I AM ALSO MAKING A LIST.

LIST OF WHAT?

A LIST OF BLIND PERSONS, JAHANPANAH.

TODAY TWO HUNDRED AND FIFTY MEN ASKED ME WHAT I WAS DOING, THOUGH I WAS WORKING IN BROAD DAYLIGHT.

OH, I SEE! BUT... WHAT'S THIS! YOU'VE GOT MY NAME HERE TOO!

YOU WERE THE LAST OF THOSE WHO ASKED ME WHAT I WAS DOING, JAHANPANAH!

HA! HA! HA! ALWAYS A WAG, EH, BIRBAL?

WHO IS GREATER?

WHEN BIRBAL ARRIVED AT COURT ONE DAY—

WATCH OUT, BIRBAL. THE KING IS IN A QUIZZING MOOD TODAY.

WHO IS GREATER, INDRA OR I?

INDRA, THE RAIN GOD, YOUR MAJESTY.

HOW DARE YOU CALL ANYONE GREATER THAN ME?

I BEG YOUR PARDON, YOUR MAJESTY.

YOU ARE GREATER THAN INDRA, O KING.

THEN YOU MUST PROVE IT!

JUST THEN BIRBAL WALKED IN—

THAT'S EASY YOUR MAJESTY!

EXPLAIN, BIRBAL.

BRAHMA THE CREATOR ALSO FACED THE SAME PROBLEM. SO HE ORDERED TWO IMAGES TO BE MADE, ONE OF YOU AND ONE OF LORD INDRA.

THEN HE ORDERED THESE TO BE PLACED ON THE CELESTIAL BALANCE TO SEE WHICH WAS GREATER.

YOUR IMAGE WAS HEAVIER, SO IT TILTED DOWN TO EARTH. INDRA'S WAS LIGHTER SO HE WENT UP.

AS A RESULT, INDRA GOT TO RULE THE HEAVENS WHILE YOU WERE MADE THE MONARCH OF THE EARTH.

HA! HA! WELL SAID, BIRBAL.

BIRBAL TO THE RESCUE
THE MASTER PSYCHOLOGIST

The route to your roots

BIRBAL TO
THE RESCUE

Pity the thief or hypocrite who crosses Birbal's path. The poor man will be either hopelessly embarrassed or pleased to escape with his life. With an unfailing eye for himan weakness, Birbal protects the innocent. People, from every strata of society, flock to him for help with endless lists of woes. Known for his compassion and tact, Birbal never fails them, even if it means pitting his wits against the all-powerful Emperor.

Script
Meera Ugra

Illustrations
Ram Waeerkar

Editor
Anant Pai

A POTFUL OF WISDOM

ONE DAY, AN ENVOY FROM THE COURT OF THE KING OF CEYLON CAME TO AKBAR'S COURT ON A STRANGE MISSION.

JAHANPANAH, YOU HAVE MANY WISE MEN AT YOUR COURT. I HAVE BEEN SENT BY MY KING TO REQUEST YOU FOR A POTFUL OF WISDOM.

A POTFUL OF WISDOM? WHAT A RIDICULOUS REQUEST!

THE KING OF CEYLON IS OUT TO BAFFLE US.

AND HE'LL SUCCEED. NO ONE, NOT EVEN BIRBAL, CAN GET US OUT OF THIS ONE.

WELL, BIRBAL?

JAHANPANAH, WE COULD EASILY SPARE SOME WISDOM.

BUT IT'LL TAKE TIME — PERHAPS A FEW WEEKS.

I'M WILLING TO WAIT.

LATER —

WELL, BIRBAL. I HOPE YOU KNOW WHAT YOU'RE DOING. OUR PRESTIGE IS AT STAKE.

DON'T WORRY, JAHANPANAH. THE KING OF CEYLON SHALL HAVE HIS POTFUL OF WISDOM.

THAT EVENING, BIRBAL SENT FOR HIS ATTENDANT.

BRING ME A FEW CLAY POTS WITH NARROW NECKS.

THE ATTENDANT SOON CAME BACK WITH THE POTS.

AH! THERE YOU ARE! GOOD. FOLLOW ME TO THE PUMPKIN PATCH.

AT THE PUMPKIN PATCH—

GIVE ME ONE OF THOSE POTS.

BIRBAL CAREFULLY PLACED THE POT OVER A PUMPKIN FLOWER.

NOW PLACE THE OTHER POTS IN THE SAME MANNER.

WHEN THE ATTENDANT FINISHED PLACING THE LAST POT—

KEEP AN EYE ON THESE, AND DON'T LET THEM BE MOVED.

I'LL HAVE THEM COLLECTED LATER.

ANY TIME, HUZUR.

A FEW WEEKS LATER —

HAVE YOU MADE ANY PROGRESS, BIRBAL?

YES, JAHANPANAH. I'M ALMOST THROUGH WITH THE TASK.

I SHOULD BE ABLE TO HAVE THE POT FILLED IN... SAY... A FORTNIGHT.

A FORTNIGHT LATER —

AHA — NOW THEY ARE ALMOST AS BIG AS THE POTS! GOOD!

YOU SHALL BE HANDSOMELY REWARDED FOR YOUR LABOUR.

LATER BIRBAL HAD THE ENVOY SUMMONED TO COURT.

THE POTFUL OF WISDOM IS READY, JAHANPANAH.

4

BIRBAL CLAPPED HIS HANDS —

THE NEXT MOMENT, HIS ATTENDANT WALKED SOLEMNLY IN, CARRYING A TRAY WITH A POT ON IT.

HERE YOU ARE. YOU MAY TAKE IT TO YOUR KING. BUT REMEMBER...

...OUR PRECIOUS POT MUST BE RETURNED EMPTY AND INTACT. AND...

...THE FRUIT OF WISDOM THAT IT CONTAINS, TO BE OF ANY VALUE, MUST BE REMOVED WITHOUT A SCRATCH!

MAY I HAVE A LOOK AT IT?

CERTAINLY.

WE HAVE FIVE MORE, IF YOUR KING NEEDS ANY MORE WISDOM.

WE ARE NO MATCH FOR BIRBAL. WHY DID WE EVER TRY!

AS SOON AS THE ENVOY LEFT—

BIRBAL, I AM CURIOUS TO HAVE A LOOK AT THE FRUIT OF WISDOM. YOU SAID YOU HAVE FIVE MORE.

I'LL HAVE THEM SENT TO YOU, JAHAN-PANAH.

WHEN THE OTHER POTS WERE BROUGHT, AKBAR LOOKED INTO ONE OF THEM...

?

HA! HA! HA! THE FRUIT OF WISDOM INDEED! IT WILL CERTAINLY MAKE THE KING OF CEYLON A WISER MAN, THOUGH!

THE EMPEROR'S TOUCH

ONE DAY, AN OLD WOMAN AND HER WIDOWED DAUGHTER-IN-LAW CAME TO BIRBAL.

MY SON HAD SERVED IN THE ROYAL ARMY FOR TWENTY YEARS. BUT NOW, HE IS DEAD AND WE HAVE NO ONE TO TURN TO!

OUR EMPEROR IS KIND AND GENEROUS. HE WILL HELP YOU. DO AS I SAY.

THE FOLLOWING DAY, AT COURT—

JAHANPANAH, THIS SWORD ONCE WIELDED BY MY SON HAS WON MANY BATTLES FOR YOU. SO, PLEASE KEEP IT IN THE ARMOURY.

LET ME SEE IT.

THE SWORD WAS HANDED OVER TO THE EMPEROR. HE EXAMINED IT CAREFULLY.

IT'S OLD AND RUSTY... OF NO USE TO US WHATSOEVER.

HE GAVE THE SWORD TO AN ATTENDANT.

RETURN IT TO HER AND GIVE HER FIVE GOLD COINS FOR HER TROUBLE.

JUST FIVE GOLD COINS!

MAY I INSPECT THE SWORD, JAHANPANAH?

BIRBAL TOOK THE SWORD...

...AND LOOKED AT IT CLOSELY...

...AGAIN AND AGAIN.

?

WHY, BIRBAL, WHAT'S WRONG?

NOTHING, JAHAN-PANAH. IT'S ONLY THAT... I WAS CONFIDENT THE SWORD WOULD HAVE TURNED GOLDEN.

TURNED GOLDEN?

YES, JAHANPANAH. WHEN EVEN THE PARAS *, A MERE STONE, CAN TRANSMUTE IRON INTO GOLD...

...I'M SURPRISED THAT WHILE PASSING THROUGH YOUR BENEVOLENT HANDS...

...WELL...

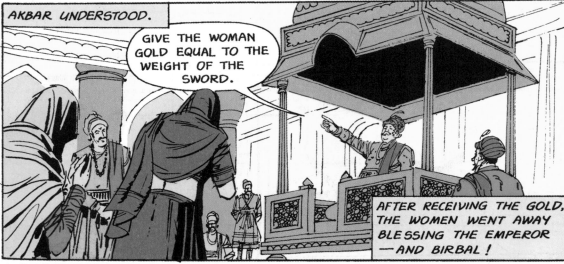

AKBAR UNDERSTOOD.

GIVE THE WOMAN GOLD EQUAL TO THE WEIGHT OF THE SWORD.

AFTER RECEIVING THE GOLD, THE WOMEN WENT AWAY BLESSING THE EMPEROR —AND BIRBAL!

* A LEGENDARY STONE CREDITED WITH THE POWER OF CHANGING IRON INTO GOLD

A WIDOW'S SAVINGS

THE RICH AND THE POOR, THE YOUNG AND THE OLD, ALL SOUGHT BIRBAL'S HELP WHEN THEY WERE WRONGED. ONE DAY AN OLD WIDOW CAME TO SEE HIM.

HELP ME, HUZUR. I'VE BEEN SWINDLED.

BY WHOM?

IT'S A LONG STORY, HUZUR. SIX MONTHS AGO, I DECIDED TO GO ON A PILGRIMAGE.

BUT I WAS WORRIED ABOUT MY MONEY. I DIDN'T KNOW WHERE TO KEEP IT.

"FINALLY, I WENT TO A MENDICANT."

HERE IS A BAG OF COPPER COINS — ALL THAT I HAVE IN THIS WORLD. PLEASE KEEP IT FOR ME. IT WILL BE SAFE WITH YOU!

I'M SORRY. I CAN'T BE INVOLVED IN WORLDLY MATTERS. I DON'T TOUCH MONEY BUT...

...YOU MAY DIG A HOLE SOMEWHERE IN MY HUT AND BURY THE BAG THERE YOURSELF.

"SO I WENT TO A CORNER OF THE HUT AND DUG A SMALL HOLE."

MY COINS WILL BE SAFE HERE.

"ON MY RETURN, WHEN I WENT TO THE MENDICANT TO COLLECT THE MONEY —"

WHAT MONEY ARE YOU TALKING ABOUT?

THE BAG OF COINS I BURIED IN YOUR HUT.

12

BUT SIR, I DID BURY IT HERE... THREE MONTHS AGO ... IN **YOUR** PRESENCE!

QUITE POSSIBLE. BUT I AM BLIND TO WHAT GOES ON IN THIS MATERIALISTIC WORLD.

MY MIND HAS ONLY ONE THOUGHT—RAMA; MY EARS HEAR ONLY ONE SOUND—RAMA; MY EYES BEHOLD BUT ONE FORM— RAMA!

I CAME AWAY. WHAT *ELSE* COULD I DO?

COULD THE MENDICANT HAVE STOLEN YOUR COINS?

I AM SURE HE HAS. BUT I HAVE NO PROOF.

HM.

14

BIRBAL WENT INTO THE HUT AND FELL PROSTRATE IN FRONT OF THE MENDICANT.

BLESS ME, MASTER.

MAY YOU LIVE LONG, MY CHILD.

I HAVE HEARD PEOPLE TALK ABOUT YOUR SPIRITUAL EMINENCE. TODAY I HAVE HAD THE GOOD FORTUNE OF RECEIVING YOUR BLESSINGS.

I WONDER WHAT HE HAS IN THE CASKET. GOLD? JEWELS?

HOLY ONE, I HATE TO TROUBLE YOU WITH THE PROBLEMS WE FOOLISH MORTALS HAVE. BUT...

SPEAK UP, CHILD. LET ME HELP YOU IF I CAN.

NO, SIR. YOU MUSTN'T. YOU ARE A MAN OF GOD. I SHOULDN'T BURDEN YOU WITH WORLDLY WORRIES.

WHAT! IS HE GOING AWAY WITH THE CASKET?

BUT... BUT WHO ELSE CAN I TRUST IN THIS WICKED, WICKED WORLD? PLEASE GUIDE ME.

HE IS WAVERING. I MUST LAY HANDS ON THAT CASKET.

I SHALL ALWAYS BE GRATEFUL TO YOU.

AH! THAT'S MY CUE.

AS THE OLD WOMAN ENTERED THE HUT —

WHY DID THIS WRETCH HAVE TO COME HERE NOW? WHAT IF SHE STARTS SHOUTING FOR HER MONEY?

SHOULD I LOSE THOSE PRECIOUS JEWELS FOR THE SAKE OF A BAG OF COPPER COINS? NO!

THANK GOD YOU'RE BACK! I'VE BEEN THINKING ABOUT YOUR BAG OF COINS. I'M SURE YOU MADE A MISTAKE THE OTHER DAY!

BUT...

SO CHILD, BURY YOUR CASKET ANYWHERE BUT DO REMEMBER THE PLACE. I DON'T UNDERSTAND ANYTHING ABOUT THESE WORLDLY MATTERS.

I CAN SEE THAT!

JUST THEN AN ATTENDANT CAME TO BIRBAL.

HUZUR, YOUR BROTHER HAS COME TO VISIT YOU! HE WANTS TO MEET YOU IMMEDIATELY.

OH, OH! SO I DON'T HAVE TO GO TO AJMER AFTER ALL!

MAY I THANK YOU FOR YOUR KINDNESS, HOLY ONE?

AND BIRBAL WALKED OUT WITH THE CASKET.

THE PERFECT PORTRAIT

ONE DAY, BIRBAL WAS SURPRISED TO FIND THE NORMALLY CHEERFUL COURT ARTIST LOOKING GLUM.

WHAT'S THE MATTER, MY FRIEND?

MY REPUTATION IS AT STAKE.

BUT YOU ARE THE BEST ARTIST THE COURT HAS EVER KNOWN. I DON'T UNDERSTAND...

YOU WILL, WHEN I'VE TOLD YOU THE WHOLE STORY.

THE ARTIST TOOK BIRBAL TO HIS HOUSE AND SHOWED HIM FIVE PORTRAITS.

THEY ARE OF A RICH NOBLE.

AREN'T THESE OF THE SAME MAN?

"A MONTH AGO HE THREW ME A CHALLENGE."

I BET, YOU CAN'T CREATE AN EXACT LIKENESS OF ME.

I BET, I CAN.

"HE POSED AND I GOT DOWN TO WORK. AT LAST —"

THAT'S ALL. I'LL GIVE THE PORTRAIT A FEW FINISHING TOUCHES AND BRING IT TO YOU TOMORROW.

"ON THE FOLLOWING DAY, WHEN I HANDED THE PORTRAIT TO HIM, CONFIDENT OF WINNING THE BET —"

THIS WON'T DO! IT ISN'T AN EXACT LIKENESS. I DON'T HAVE A BEARD!

BUT YOU DID HAVE ONE WHEN YOU POSED FOR THE PORTRAIT!

A BET IS A BET! AND AN EXACT LIKENESS AN EXACT LIKENESS! HERE! YOU MAY KEEP THIS AS A MEMENTO.

PLEASE GIVE ME ANOTHER CHANCE.

ALL RIGHT. YOU MAY TRY AGAIN.

CALM YOURSELF, MY FRIEND. ALL IS NOT LOST! DO AS I TELL YOU AND YOU'LL HAVE THE LAST LAUGH!

A FEW DAYS LATER —

OH, IT'S YOU AGAIN! WHAT HAVE YOU COME WITH NOW? ANOTHER USE- LESS PORTRAIT?

WHEN THE NOBLE UNWRAPPED THE PARCEL —

A MIRROR!

HOW DARE YOU PLAY GAMES WITH ME! THIS IS NO PORTRAIT! IT'S...

AN EXACT LIKENESS OF YOURSELF! ISN'T THAT WHAT YOU WANTED, MY FRIEND?

THE NOBLE SHEEPISHLY ACCEPTED DEFEAT AND THE ARTIST BECAME HIS CHEER- FUL SELF AGAIN.

SPEAK THE TRUTH BUT MAKE IT PLEASANT

THERE HE IS! AT IT AGAIN!

IF BIRBAL'S NEIGHBOUR HAD A WEAKNESS, IT WAS TO HAVE HIS FORTUNE TOLD.

SUDDENLY —

YOU FRAUD! DON'T YOU DARE COME THIS WAY AGAIN!

I WON'T! EVER!

BIRBAL WENT UP TO THE MAN.

WHAT DID YOU DO TO MAKE HIM SO ANGRY?

I READ HIS HOROSCOPE AND PREDICTED THAT HIS NEAR AND DEAR ONES WOULD DIE BEFORE HIM. AND THEN...

HE THREW YOU OUT, DIDN'T HE?

HE DID. HE COULDN'T FACE THE TRUTH, AND...

...I COULDN'T LIE.

YOU DID WELL TO SPEAK THE TRUTH BUT...

...YOU COULD HAVE MADE IT MORE PLEASANT!

PLEASANT? I DON'T UNDERSTAND. HOW...

IT'S SIMPLE. I'LL TELL YOU HOW. LISTEN...

...NOW DO AS I'VE TOLD YOU, AND SEE HOW HE RESPONDS. DON'T FORGET THE DISGUISE!

THE NEXT DAY —

AH, SIR! WHAT A STRIKING PERSONALITY YOU HAVE! MAY I READ YOUR PALM?

CERTAINLY, CERTAINLY, GOOD SIR!

WHAT A GLORIOUS FUTURE! AND WHAT A LONG LIFE! IN FACT...

...YOU'LL LIVE LONGER THAN ALL YOUR NEAR AND DEAR ONES!

REALLY? AND THAT RASCAL SAID YESTERDAY THAT...

NEVER MIND! WHY TALK OF INAUSPICIOUS MATTERS AT THIS AUSPICIOUS MOMENT? WAIT. I HAVE SOMETHING FOR YOU.

HE WENT IN AND CAME OUT WITH A BAG OF COINS.

DO COME AGAIN WHENEVER YOU HAVE THE TIME.

I WILL. MOST CERTAINLY!

LATER —

I NEVER DREAMT, HUZUR, THAT THE MANNER IN WHICH I WORD MY READING IS EVEN MORE IMPORTANT THAN THE READING ITSELF!

THE HOLY PARROT

ONE DAY, AKBAR'S FAVOURITE ATTENDANT CAME TO BIRBAL. HE WAS ALMOST IN TEARS.

HUZUR! HUZUR! YOU'VE GOT TO HELP ME! ONLY YOU CAN SAVE MY LIFE. I.... THE EMPEROR...

YES... GO ON...

"A FEW MONTHS AGO, THE EMPEROR GAVE ME A PARROT."

IT'S A VERY SPECIAL BIRD; A HOLY MAN'S GIFT TO ME. TAKE GOOD CARE OF IT.

SHOULD ANYONE BRING ME NEWS OF ITS DEATH, I'LL BEHEAD HIM!

AND NOW... AND NOW IN SPITE OF MY LOVING CARE, IT SUDDENLY DIED. WHAT SHALL I DO?

IS THAT ALL? LEAVE IT TO ME. I'LL TAKE THE NEWS TO THE EMPEROR, AND YET SAVE MY HEAD!

LATER, AT AKBAR'S COURT —

JAHANPANAH, DO YOU REMEMBER THE PARROT THAT FAKIR GAVE YOU? IT'S A HOLY BIRD INDEED!

A HOLY BIRD, INDEED. HA! HA! HA!

IT IS, JAHANPANAH. I HAD GONE TO SEE IT. AND WHAT DO YOU THINK IT WAS DOING?

MEDITATING! WITH ITS EYES CLOSED AND ITS HEAD TURNED SKY-WARDS!

YOU MUST BE JOKING.

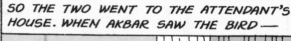

SO THE TWO WENT TO THE ATTENDANT'S HOUSE. WHEN AKBAR SAW THE BIRD —

BIRBAL YOU MAY BE WISE, AND CLEVER! BUT THERE IS A LIMIT.

THIS BIRD IS DEAD! AND DON'T TELL ME YOU DIDN'T KNOW IT.

I DID. BUT I DIDN'T WANT TO BE BEHEADED!

ONLY THEN DID AKBAR REMEMBER WHAT HE HAD TOLD HIS ATTENDANT.

WELL! WELL! WELL! YOU'VE SAVED YET ANOTHER HEAD, BIRBAL. AND I'M GRATEFUL TO YOU FOR IT.

AKBAR THE HUNTER

AKBAR WAS EXTREMELY FOND OF HUNTING. ONE DAY—

HELP US, HUZOOR!

OUR VILLAGE IS BEING RAZED!

WHY ON EARTH?

THE KING WANTS MORE FORESTS IN HIS KINGDOM.

HIS MEN HAVE ORDERS TO CREATE MORE AND MORE NEW FORESTS

THE KING WANTS NEW JUNGLES TO HUNT IN.

I'LL TRY AND DO WHAT I CAN.

ON THE NEXT HUNTING TRIP—

AH! THIS IS SO EXHILARATING. DON'T YOU THINK SO, BIRBAL?

UH, HUH!

LOOK AT THOSE OWLS!

CHI-CHI-THUP-THUP

THE TWO GROUPS SEEM TO BE HAVING A QUARREL.

BIRBAL IS SO WISE. HE SHOULD BE ABLE TO MAKE OUT WHAT THEY ARE SAYING

YES, BIRBAL. TELL US WHY THEY ARE FIGHTING

I COULD TELL YOU BUT...

WHY DO YOU HESITATE?

YOUR MAJESTY MAY NOT LIKE TO HEAR IT

GO ON WHY SHOULD I MIND WHAT THE BIRDS SAY?

A GROUP OF OWLS HAVE COME FROM THE NEIGHBOURING KINGDOM TO MARRY ONE OF THEIR BOYS TO A GIRL OWL HERE.

THEY ARE ARRANGING FOR THE MARRIAGE. BUT THERE IS A DISPUTE BETWEEN THE GROOM'S FATHER AND THE BRIDE'S FATHER.

WHY?

THE BOY'S FATHER IS DEMANDING A GIFT OF FORTY FORESTS. BUT THE GIRL'S FATHER IS SAYING HE CANNOT COMPLY NOW...

... HOWEVER, AFTER A FEW YEARS, HE PROMISES TO GIFT EIGHTY FORESTS TO THE COUPLE.

HOW? IF HE DOESN'T HAVE FORTY FORESTS NOW, HOW WILL HE GIVE DOUBLE THE NUMBER LATER?

WELL, HE SAYS THE EMPEROR HERE IS VERY FOND OF HUNTING.

HE KEEPS CONVERTING VILLAGES INTO JUNGLES FOR HIS HUNTING PLEASURE SO THE NUMBER OF FORESTS IS SURE TO DOUBLE IN THE FUTURE.

AKBAR UNDERSTOOD THE MESSAGE BIRBAL WAS TRYING TO CONVEY.

YOU ARE RIGHT, BIRBAL. IT IS SELFISH OF ME TO DESTROY VILLAGE AFTER VILLAGE FOR MY HUNTING PLEASURE.